D1207569

EYES ON
ANIMALS

Courtney Acampora

Silver Dolphin

Silver Dolphin Books
An imprint of Printers Row Publishing Group
A division of Readerlink Distribution Services, LLC
10350 Barnes Canyon Road, Suite 100, San Diego, CA 92121
www.silverdolphinbooks.com

Copyright © 2018 Silver Dolphin Books
All rights reserved. No part of this publication may be reproduced, distributed, or transmitted in any form or by any means, including photocopying, recording, or other electronic or mechanical methods, without the prior written permission of the publisher, except in the case of brief quotations embodied in critical reviews and certain other noncommercial uses permitted by copyright law.

Printers Row Publishing Group is a division of Readerlink Distribution Services, LLC.

Silver Dolphin Books is a registered trademark of Readerlink Distribution Services, LLC.

All notations of errors or omissions should be addressed to Silver Dolphin Books, Editorial Department, at the above address.

Written by Courtney Acampora
Designed by Haydee Yanez

ISBN: 978-1-68412-312-4
Manufactured, printed, and assembled Heshan, China. First printing, May 2018. HH/05/18.
22 21 20 19 18   1 2 3 4 5

Image Credits: Getty Images

CONTENTS

AMAZING

From snowcapped mountains to scorching deserts, amazing animals can be found in every habitat around the world. From a distance, they can be seen on the prowl, hidden in the trees, or submerged in water. But up close, these animals have extraordinary features that make them master hunters, help camouflage them in their surroundings, and stay safe from predators.

ANIMALS
AROUND THE WORLD

Whether it's the striped tiger, colorful macaw, or masked raccoon, get ready for a one-of-a-kind peek at some of the world's most fascinating creatures.

KING OF THE JUNGLE

Although lions are often called "kings of the jungle," tigers are the actual kings of this habitat! They are the largest cats in the wild, with powerful roars that can be heard from a mile away. Unlike most cats around the world, tigers actually enjoy swimming and can swim long distances or just go in for a refreshing dip.

Like a human's thumbprint, each tiger has a unique striped pattern. Although it seems like the orange, black, and white stripes would make a tiger stand out in the wild, this specialized coloring actually helps tigers blend into the splotchy and shadowy forest. Their camouflage helps them ambush their predators; they quietly and unsuspectedly pounce on passing prey by using their powerful jaws and claws.

QUICK STATS

HABITAT:
Jungles and forests of Asia

FOOD:
Deer, pigs, buffalo

SIZE:
Up to 10 feet long

WEIGHT:
Up to 660 pounds

LIFE EXPECTANCY:
10 years

How Do You Feel?
Like domestic cats, tigers have whiskers that help them detect danger or prey. Their whiskers are located in five areas on their bodies: nose, above the eyes, cheeks, behind the front legs, and throughout their body fur.

THE REAL KING KONG

QUICK STATS

HABITAT:
Forests of central Africa

FOOD:
Roots, fruit, tree bark

SIZE:
4–6 feet

WEIGHT:
300–485 pounds

LIFE EXPECTANCY:
Up to 35 years

High in the misty mountains of central Africa, mountain gorillas live in large family groups. Each group, or troop, of gorillas is led by a male called a silverback. Around 12 to 15 years old, male gorillas develop a distinctive silver coloring on their backs. The troop consists of mostly female gorillas and their young. Like human children, young gorillas love to play and enjoy wrestling, chasing one another, and swinging on tree branches. Gorillas spend most of their day eating plants. Since a troop can go through so much food, each day gorillas move to a new area in the forest to settle and eat for the day.

One of a Kind

From the outside, all gorillas may look the same, but there are several clues on their bodies that truly make them one of a kind. Like humans, gorillas have unique fingerprints and toe prints. In addition, each gorilla's nose is unique. In fact, scientists often distinguish one gorilla from another by looking at their nose!

A FLYING
RAINBOW

Blue, red, yellow, green. Looking up from the rain forest floor, one may think they're looking at a moving rainbow! Macaws are part of the parrot family, and although their bright colors may seem to make them stand out, their colorful feathers actually help them blend in among the colorful fruits and flowers of the rain forest.

Their strong beaks are used to break into their favorite foods: fruits and nuts. Macaws also use their strong toes to grip onto branches and hold their food.

QUICK STATS

HABITAT:
Rain forests

FOOD:
Seeds, nuts, insects

SIZE:
Up to 39.5 inches

WEIGHT:
Up to 3.75 pounds

LIFE EXPECTANCY:
Up to 60 years

Rain Forest Families

Once macaws choose a partner, they typically stay together for life. Pairs of macaws live in larger groups, or flocks, of up to 30 birds. In addition to breeding, macaw pairs share food and groom each other's feathers. They are very vocal birds that use calls to communicate with their partner and the larger flock. Macaw pairs have such a strong bond that even in a flock they fly so close to one another that their wings practically touch!

IN THE
SHADOWS

The jaguar is the largest cat in the Americas and can be found from Mexico to Argentina. This cat is recognizable by its orange fur and black "rosette" spots. Some jaguars, however, also have black fur with black spots that are easiest to see up close. The black species of jaguar is often mistaken as a panther, but there is actually not a panther species. "Panther" is an umbrella term that refers to any big cat such as jaguars, mountain lions, and leopards.

QUICK STATS

HABITAT:
Rain forest, swamps, deserts of North America, Central America, and South America

FOOD:
Turtles, tapirs, deer, cattle, capybaras, caimans

SIZE:
Up to 6 feet long

WEIGHT:
Up to 250 pounds

LIFE EXPECTANCY:
Up to 15 years

Pouncing Predator

Hiding in the shadowed rain forest, jaguars are ambush hunters that don't chase their prey, but rather wait for the opportunity to strike. The word "jaguar" comes from the Native American word "yaguar," which means "he who kills with one leap." In addition to leaping on their prey, jaguars are excellent swimmers, which is useful because most of their prey lives in the water!

KING OF THE SAVANNA

The most social of the cat family, lions live in groups, called prides, of up to 15 lions. Within the pride, the lions work together to hunt, raise cubs, and defend their territory.

The female lions, or lionesses, are usually all related and are mothers, daughters, grandmothers, or sisters. The lionesses raise the cubs and hunt while the two male lions in the pride defend their territory. Like domestic cats, lions are great climbers, purr, lick each other's fur, and rub heads with other lions.

QUICK STATS

HABITAT:
African savanna

FOOD:
Antelope, wildebeest, zebras

SIZE:
Females up to 5.5 feet, males up to 8 feet

WEIGHT:
Up to 420 pounds

LIFE EXPECTANCY:
Up to 14 years

The Mane Man

One of the most obvious differences between male and female lions are the manes featured around the male's head. The mane not only makes the male look bigger, but it also protects the lion's neck from the claws and teeth of other males. A lion's age can also be estimated by looking at its mane—the darker the mane, the older the male.

BIG BIRD

The tallest and heaviest bird in the world, the ostrich is too big to fly, but can run up to 43 mph at short distances, and 30 mph at long distances. Each stride can be as long as 16 feet. They hold their wings out for balance as they run. Ostriches' strong legs not only help them run fast, but they are also used as a defense mechanism. A 4-inch sharp claw is located on each foot, and their kicks are so powerful, they can kill a lion!

QUICK STATS

HABITAT:
African grasslands

FOOD:
Insects, seeds, leaves, roots

SIZE:
Up to 9 feet tall

WEIGHT:
Up to 350 pounds

LIFE EXPECTANCY:
Up to 40 years

Hatchin' a Plan

Ostrich eggs are the largest eggs of any animal in the world. They are approximately 6 inches in length, 5 inches in width, and weigh up to 6 pounds. Ostriches live in groups of up to 12. All of the females lay their eggs in one communal nest. Each female can lay up to 7 to10 eggs at a time. When the eggs hatch, the chicks are small and fluffy, and after only a few days, they can walk and follow their mothers.

GENTLE
GIANTS

Babar, Dumbo, Horton—it's no wonder elephants are one of the most popular animals in the world. When they aren't portrayed in cartoons, elephants live in herds on the African grasslands. Herds consist of related females and their babies; males do not live in herds.

Elephants are known for having a long trunk, which acts as a useful arm, hand, nose, and mouth! Trunks do not have any bones or cartilage, but they are strong enough to grab, pull, touch, reach, and throw. The end of the trunk has two holes used for breathing and for sucking up water—
like a straw!

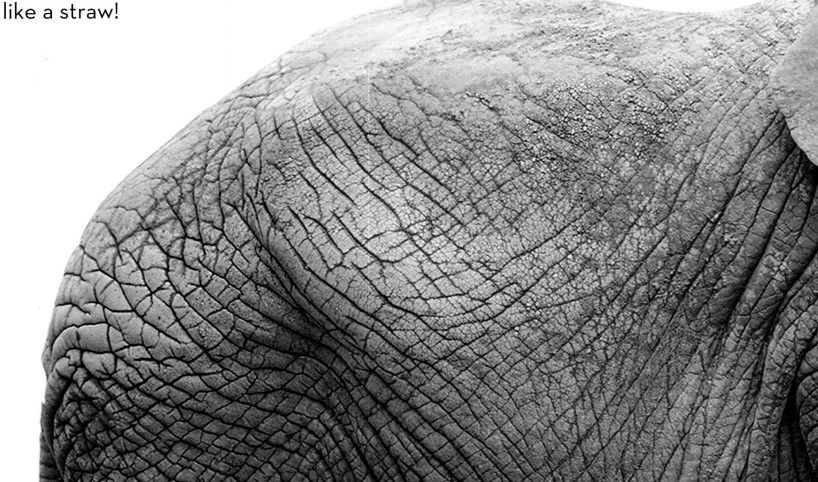

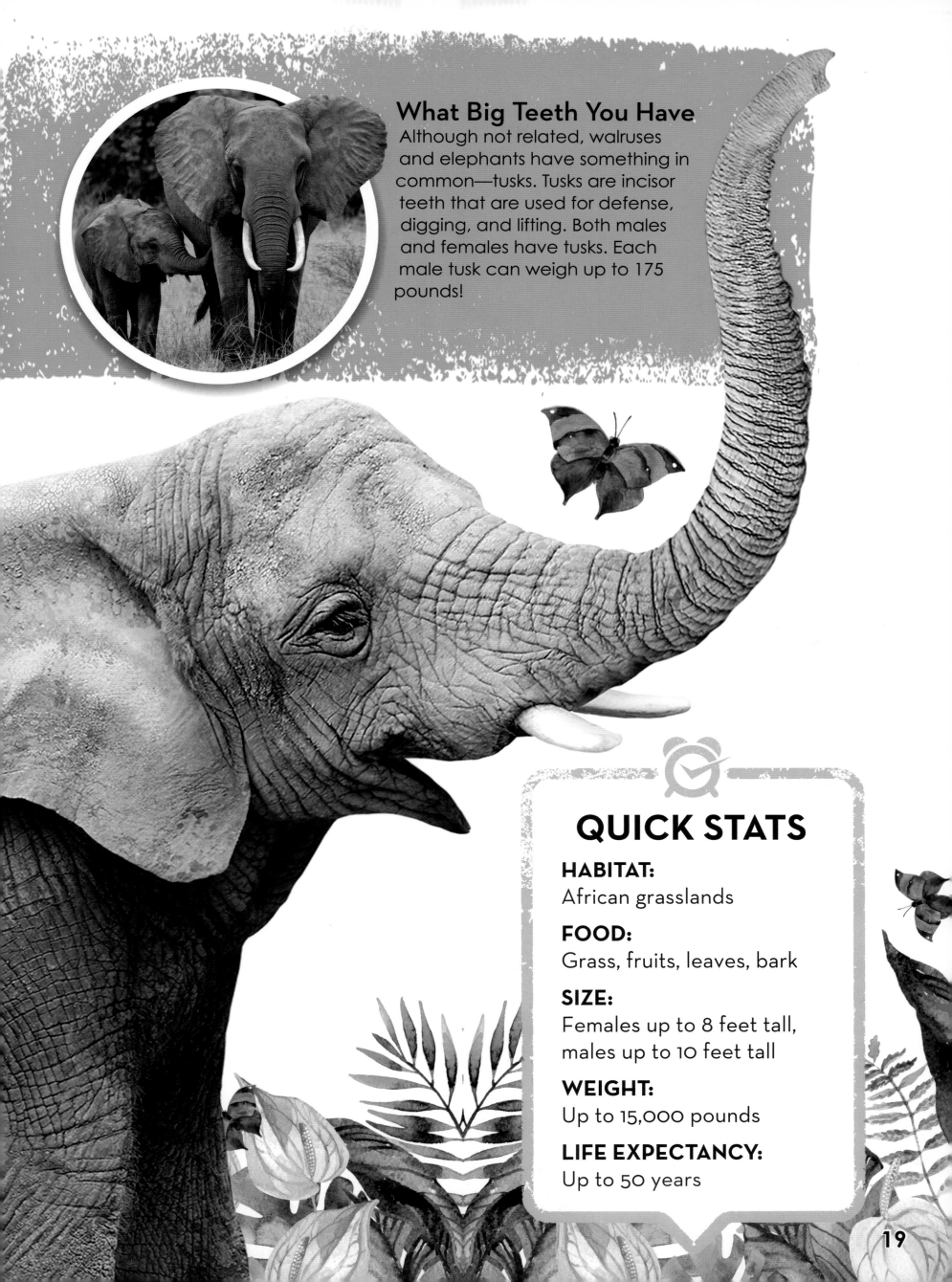

What Big Teeth You Have

Although not related, walruses and elephants have something in common—tusks. Tusks are incisor teeth that are used for defense, digging, and lifting. Both males and females have tusks. Each male tusk can weigh up to 175 pounds!

QUICK STATS

HABITAT:
African grasslands

FOOD:
Grass, fruits, leaves, bark

SIZE:
Females up to 8 feet tall, males up to 10 feet tall

WEIGHT:
Up to 15,000 pounds

LIFE EXPECTANCY:
Up to 50 years

WATER HORSE

QUICK STATS

HABITAT:
African savanna

FOOD:
Grasses

SIZE:
10.8–16.5 feet long

WEIGHT:
Females up to 3,000 pounds, males up to 9,000 pounds

LIFE EXPECTANCY:
Up to 36 years

Hippopotamus is a Greek word meaning "water horses." These aquatic giants may look cute, but they are one of the most dangerous animals in the world. They are extremely aggressive and will charge at anything they see as a threat. Their large mouths also have large, sharp teeth. They spend most of their day cooling off from the hot African sun in pools, rivers, and mud holes. And although they spend so much time in water, hippos can't actually swim. Instead, they gently bounce off the bottom of the lake on their tippy toes and gallop through the water. Hippos live in groups of up to 30, and while in the water their bodies appear like little islands—inviting birds and turtles to hang out on their backs and enjoy the sun.

Made for the Water

Hippos are well-equipped for life in water. Their eyes, ears, and nostrils are positioned high on their head so when they are submerged, these body parts can stay out of the water. Hippos also have built-in goggles! A clear membrane covers their eyes, which can remain open while they're under water. And their nostrils can close up, keeping water out of their nose.

STANDING TALL

Towering over the African savanna are the tallest animals in the world: giraffes. These graceful giants can be seen in groups of up to fifteen, appropriately called "towers." Giraffes are sustained by one food: acacia leaves. Their long necks help them reach acacia leaves high in the treetops. Their height is also useful for looking out for predators such as lions or hyenas. Even though they have such long necks, giraffes only have seven vertebrae—the same amount as most mammals. The difference is the size of each of the giraffe's vertebrae. Each vertebrae measures around seven inches in length.

In addition to its height, a giraffe's 21-inch long tongue also comes in handy for reaching leaves. Giraffes can go several days without water since they get much of their water from acacia leaves.

QUICK STATS

HABITAT:
African savanna

FOOD:
Acacia leaves

SIZE:
Females 14 feet tall, males 18 feet tall

WEIGHT:
Females 1,500 pounds, males 3,000 pounds

LIFE EXPECTANCY:
Up to 25 years

Head to Head

One of the most noticeable parts of a giraffe are the two knobs on its head. Both male and female giraffes have these knobs, called ossicones. Baby giraffes are born with soft ossicones that harden or "ossify" as they get older. Males use their ossicones to spar and head butt other males while fighting.

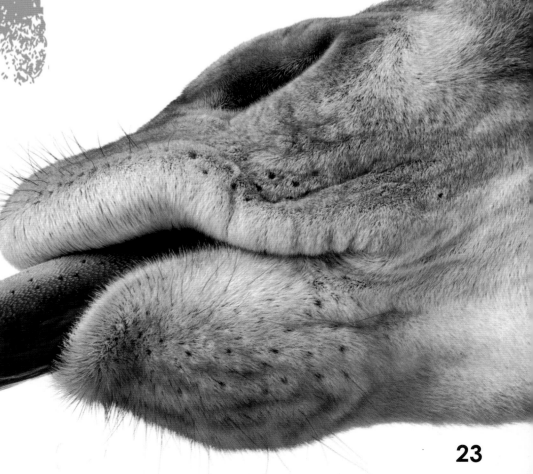

QUICK STATS

HABITAT:
African grasslands

FOOD:
Hares, antelope, warthogs, springboks

SIZE:
4 feet long with a 2.5 feet long tail

WEIGHT:
Up to 143 pounds

LIFE EXPECTANCY:
Up to 12 years

Cute and Cuddly Cubs

Baby cheetahs, called cubs, are born in litters of 3 to 5. They are born with their distinctive spots and a long stripe of silver fur, called a mantle, that grows down their back. Many cheetah cubs are prey to large predators, so the mantle helps them blend in better with the grass. As they get older, the cubs lose their mantle. When the cubs are around 6 months old, their mother teaches them to hunt and avoid predators.

SPOTTED
SPRINTERS

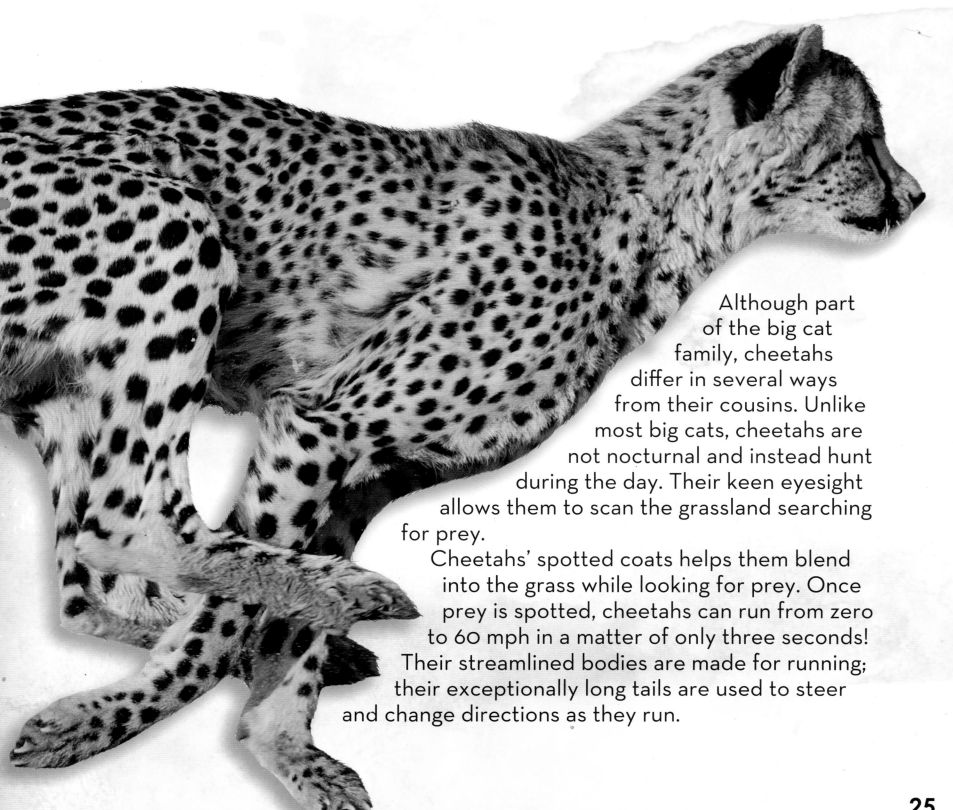

Although part of the big cat family, cheetahs differ in several ways from their cousins. Unlike most big cats, cheetahs are not nocturnal and instead hunt during the day. Their keen eyesight allows them to scan the grassland searching for prey.

Cheetahs' spotted coats helps them blend into the grass while looking for prey. Once prey is spotted, cheetahs can run from zero to 60 mph in a matter of only three seconds! Their streamlined bodies are made for running; their exceptionally long tails are used to steer and change directions as they run.

The white rhinoceros is the second-largest land mammal after elephants. Because of their large, armored body and two horns on their head, they may look frightening, but white rhinos are mostly harmless creatures that only eat grasses and plants. During the day, they're often seen lying in the shade or taking a dip in a water hole. To protect their skin from the sun and insect bites, white rhinos cover themselves in mud.

BODY OF ARMOR

QUICK STATS

HABITAT:
Grasslands of South Africa, Zimbabwe, Namibia, and Kenya

FOOD:
Grasses

SIZE:
13.75 feet long

WEIGHT:
4 tons

LIFE EXPECTANCY:
Up to 40 years

Two Horns are Better than One

White rhinos have two horns on the front of their head. The front horn is larger, with a smaller horn behind it. The front horn is used for digging for water and plants. The horns are not attached to the skull but can break off and regrow.

27

FLIPPING OUT

Green sea turtles are the largest sea turtles, and their name may cause some confusion. Green sea turtles are typically brown or black in color, and the "green" portion of their name refers to their internal skin color, which is, in fact, green. Green sea turtles can hold their breath for hours, but must come up eventually for oxygen. They are able to consume salt water because special glands in their body filter out the salt. Their flippers are paddle-shaped and help them move swiftly through the water.

Take a Long Trip

Green sea turtle mothers swim very long distances from their feeding to nesting sites. They can be found swimming in the sea except for at birth or while nesting. Once they reach the nesting site, the mother crawls onto a sandy beach, digs a deep hole, and places 100 to 200 eggs in the hole. After covering up the eggs with sand, the mother returns to sea. About two months later, the babies emerge from their shells and make their way into the ocean.

QUICK STATS

HABITAT:
Tropical and subtropical coastal waters around the world

FOOD:
Sea grasses, algae

SIZE:
5-foot-long shell

WEIGHT:
700 pounds

LIFE EXPECTANCY:
80 years

QUICK STATS

HABITAT:
Tropical and temperate coastal waters around the world

FOOD:
Crustaceans, plankton

SIZE:
Up to 14 inches

WEIGHT:
7 ounces

LIFE EXPECTANCY:
5 years

Baby Pouch

Male and female sea horses pair for life. But unlike almost all other species in the world, the male gives birth to the babies. Male sea horses have pouches of the front of their bodies that females put their eggs in. The male carries around the eggs, protecting them until the eggs hatch and the tiny baby sea horses are released in their full form!

SEA HORSING AROUND

Sea horses are some of the most unique fish in the sea. Unlike other fish, sea horses are not covered in scales, but rather a hard exoskeleton. Even though their home is in the sea, sea horses are poor swimmers. They propel themselves forward by the small fin on their back, which flutters 35 times per second.

Since they are unable to swim strongly or quickly, sea horses wrap their curly tails around sea grasses to make sure they don't wash away with the current. Sea horses can also change their color to blend into their surroundings.

Hide-And-Seek

During the day, it is common to just see an eel's head poking out from a crevice or hole in a reef. Eels are nocturnal and leave their hiding spot to hunt. When they do come across prey, they use their powerful jaws to capture their food. They have poor eyesight, but their strong sense of smell helps them find prey.

SLITHERY
LIKE SNAKES

QUICK STATS

HABITAT:
Tropical and subtropical oceans

FOOD:
Small fish, octopuses, crustaceans, shrimp, crabs

SIZE:
5 feet long

WEIGHT:
30 pounds

LIFE EXPECTANCY:
Up to 50 years

With their long bodies and sharp teeth, moray eels look like snakes of the sea. They have muscular bodies that allow them to twist and turn similarly to how snakes slither on land.

Moray eels may appear scary because their mouths are always open revealing their sharp teeth. This is because moray eels don't have gills to breathe through like other fish. Instead, they must open and close their mouths constantly in order to breathe. In addition, unlike other fish, moray eels don't have scales. They are covered in a special mucus that protects their bodies from any sharp edges that their bodies may come into contact with.

QUICK STATS

HABITAT:
Pacific, Atlantic, and Indian Oceans

FOOD:
Seals, sea lions, dolphins, fish

SIZE:
20 feet long

WEIGHT:
Up to 2.5 tons

LIFE EXPECTANCY:
70 years

With their gigantic bodies, speed, and mouths full of up to 300 razor-sharp teeth, it's no surprise that great white sharks have inspired so many scary movies. Great white sharks are one of the most ferocious predators in the world's oceans. Their speed—up to 35 mph—allows great white sharks to quickly catch prey. Then they sink in their sharp, serrated teeth to grab ahold of their dinner. And while humans are fearful of the possibility of sharks while swimming in the ocean, shark attacks are relatively rare. In fact, humans are sharks' most dangerous predators, killing approximately 100 million sharks a year.

Super Senses

Part of what makes great white sharks one of the most powerful predators are their many keen senses. Their sense of smell allows them to smell one drop of blood in 25 gallons of water. Their sense of hearing helps them sense vibrations in the water. Great white sharks also have very strong vision. Their retinas are actually divided into two parts: one for day vision and one for night vision. A sensitive line down their back senses the movement in the water created by prey. Finally, they have a special electrical sense that helps them navigate and migrate by following Earth's magnetic field.

JAW-SOME SHARKS

CLOWNING AROUND

Among the colorful coral reefs in warm oceans around the world, small orange, black, and white striped fish can be seen surrounded by poisonous sea anemones.

Clown fish are covered in a special mucus that protects them from the sea anemone's toxins. This is useful because clown fish and sea anemones have a symbiotic relationship, meaning that they are two different species that both benefit from living close to one another. For clown fish, they are able to hide among the sea anemone, which protects them from predators that are not immune to the sea anemone's poison. In return, the sea anemone gets to eat the clown fish's scraps and is cleaned by the clown fish.

Male or Female?

Clown fish are one of the few anomalies in nature—all are born male, and later in life can change into females. Inside each sea anemone, there is a hierarchy with a dominant female clown fish, then the male clown fish, and then their offspring. If the alpha female dies, then the male can change into a female. Because clown fish rarely leave their sea anemone, it would be difficult to find another female so their ability to change sex allows them to breed without leaving the comfort of their home.

QUICK STATS

HABITAT:
Indian Ocean, Red Sea, western Pacific Ocean

FOOD:
Algae, zooplankton, worms, small crustaceans

SIZE:
4.3 inches long

WEIGHT:
9 ounces

LIFE EXPECTANCY:
Up to 10 years

ALL PUFFED UP

QUICK STATS

HABITAT:
Oceans around the world

FOOD:
Snails, shellfish, crustaceans

SIZE:
Up to 3 feet long

WEIGHT:
Up to 30 pounds

LIFE EXPECTANCY:
Up to 8 years

Wink, Wink
Their unique ability to change their body shape isn't the only thing that makes puffer fish unlike other fish in the ocean. Puffer fish are scale-less, and they are some of the only known fish with the ability to close and blink their eyes!

One minute they're small, and the next minute they can be several times larger than their normal size! Puffer fish are some of the most transformable fish in the sea. Because they are slow and clumsy swimmers, their main defense mechanism is to inflate into a ball. Puffer fish have elastic stomachs that allow them to gulp large amounts of water so they puff up and are more difficult for predators to eat. Some species of puffer fish have spines on their backs that also protect them. They not only inflate into spiny balls, but puffer fish also have a toxic substance that makes them taste bad to predators and be potentially deadly. One particular puffer fish has enough poison to kill 30 adult humans!

DARLING DOLPHINS

Dolphins are mammals like humans, meaning they give birth to live young, feed their babies milk, and must come out of the water to breathe. They are also like humans in that they like to play! Dolphins live in pods of up to 15 dolphins and enjoy chasing one another, leaping out of the water, splashing, doing somersaults, and even playing with seaweed, coral, and bubbles.

They are intelligent creatures that use tools like primates. Dolphins have been seen grasping sea sponges in their mouth as they forage for food. While searching rocks and the seafloor for food, the sponge acts as a barrier and prevents any cuts and scrapes on the dolphin's nose.

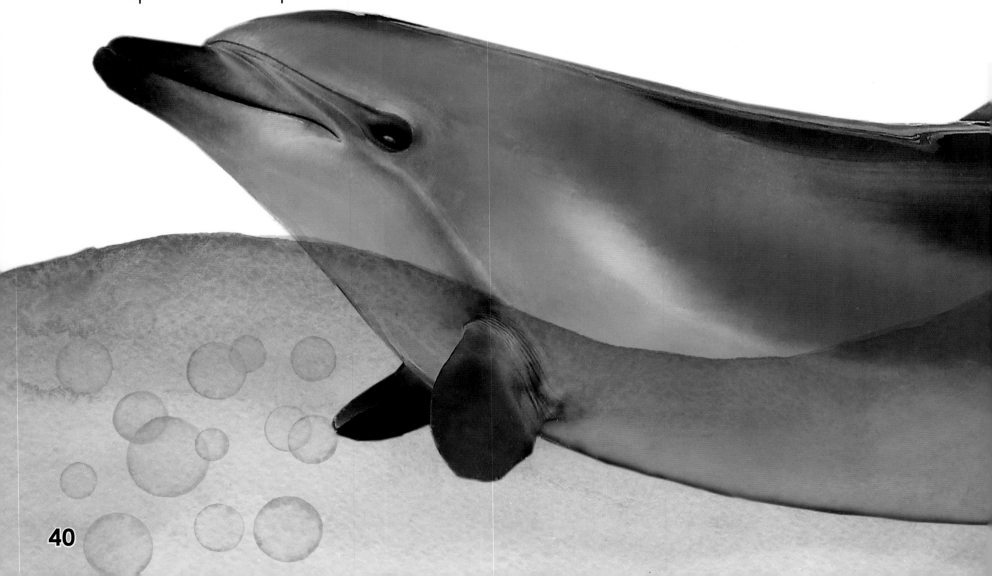

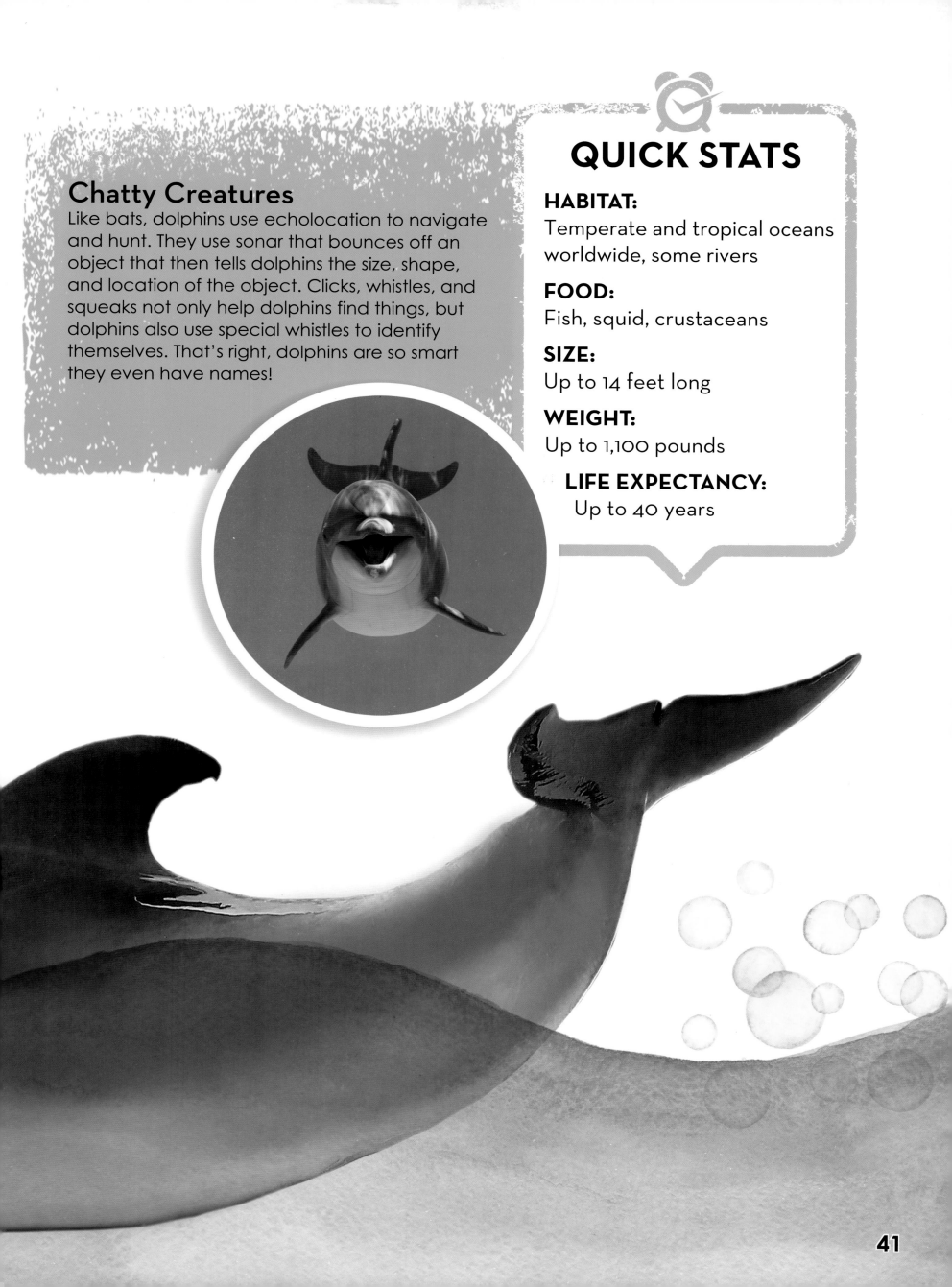

Chatty Creatures

Like bats, dolphins use echolocation to navigate and hunt. They use sonar that bounces off an object that then tells dolphins the size, shape, and location of the object. Clicks, whistles, and squeaks not only help dolphins find things, but dolphins also use special whistles to identify themselves. That's right, dolphins are so smart they even have names!

QUICK STATS

HABITAT:
Temperate and tropical oceans worldwide, some rivers

FOOD:
Fish, squid, crustaceans

SIZE:
Up to 14 feet long

WEIGHT:
Up to 1,100 pounds

LIFE EXPECTANCY:
Up to 40 years

QUICK STATS

HABITAT:
Cold seas and ice in Antarctica

FOOD:
Krill, fish, squid

SIZE:
Up to 3.7 feet tall

WEIGHT:
Up to 90 pounds

LIFE EXPECTANCY:
Up to 20 years

Bundle Up, Baby!

When they aren't swimming, emperor penguins congregate in large groups called colonies. Female emperor penguins lay one egg, then leave the egg with the male while she searches for food. The male emperor penguin rests the egg on his feet and covers the egg with a flap of belly skin that keeps the egg warm. Males often gather close together to keep the eggs warm. The female then returns once the egg hatches, allowing the male to search for food.

They may look like they're dressed in a tuxedo for a fancy ball, but emperor penguins' distinctive black and white coloring has an important function. Called countershading, emperor penguins' white bellies make them more difficult to see by predators below them in the water, and their black backs camouflage them from predators looking down at them in the water. This camouflage is especially important for penguins because they spend 75 percent of their time in the water searching for food. Although they're birds, penguins can't fly. Instead, they use their wings and webbed feet to swiftly swim in the water, catching fish and swallowing them whole.

ALL
DRESSED
UP

RULE THE ICE

Way up in the Arctic, polar bears rule the ice . . . and water. When they aren't sleeping up to 20 hours a day, polar bears hunt through cracks in the ice or breathing holes. They are also excellent swimmers that can swim up to 60 miles looking for food. Polar bears use their large paws to paddle through the water, and they have a special membrane that covers their eyes so they can see underwater. They can also smell their favorite food, seals, from up to 20 miles away.

QUICK STATS

HABITAT:
Arctic

FOOD:
Seals

SIZE:
Females 8 feet long, males 10 feet long

WEIGHT:
Females 650 pounds, males 1,200 pounds

LIFE EXPECTANCY:
Up to 24 years

Made for the Cold

Although polar bear fur may appear white, each hair is actually a hollow, clear tube. Their white coloring camouflages them against the snow and ice. Their dense, insulated fur and layer of fat keeps them warm in the chilly Arctic. Polar bears also have small bumps and fur on their paws that help them grip the slick ice.

Way up in the Arctic Circle, lumbering, cinnamon-colored creatures sun on the ice. These massive creatures are walruses, and they are very social animals that gather in groups. When they aren't making a variety of noisy snorts and bellows, walruses dive deep in the sea for up to ten minutes without air.

Walrus faces feature whiskers that sense vibrations in the water, which are useful when they are deep down in the ocean looking for shellfish. Their whiskers are as sensitive as human fingers and allow the walrus to find food in the dark.

Tooth-Walking Sea Horse

It may sound strange, but "walrus" in Latin translates to "tooth-walking sea horse"! "Tooth-walking" refers to the long tusks that grow out of both males' and females' mouths that help them move across the ice and lift them out of the water. Walruses also use their tusks to break holes in the ice so they can look for food. Their tusks grow throughout their lives and can grow to be three feet long!

QUICK STATS

HABITAT:
Arctic Circle

FOOD:
Clams, mussels, shellfish

SIZE:
Up to 11 feet long

WEIGHT:
Up to 3,000 pounds

LIFE EXPECTANCY:
Up to 40 years

WALLOWING WALRUSES

ALL BUNDLED UP

Arctic foxes are well-adapted for life in the freezing Arctic tundra. During winter when the landscape is covered in snow, Arctic foxes' fur turns white so they can blend into their surroundings.

Once the snow has melted in the spring revealing the tundra's gray and brown rocks and plants, the Arctic foxes' fur turns brownish-gray. In order to survive the winter's freezing temperatures, Arctic foxes have short muzzles, small ears, and thick fur that minimize heat loss. To keep warm, their long, fluffy tail, called a brush, is also used to wrap around their bodies like a scarf.

QUICK STATS

HABITAT:
Tundra in Alaska, Canada, Greenland, Iceland, northern Europe, Russia

FOOD:
Lemmings, squirrels, birds, eggs, berries, fish

SIZE:
26-inch body with a 13-inch tail

WEIGHT:
17 pounds

LIFE EXPECTANCY:
6 years

Time to Eat!
Arctic foxes have a keen sense of smell and hearing used for finding prey. The Arctic fox leaps into the air and lands straight down on its prey. In the winter, when prey is scarce, Arctic foxes trail behind polar bears to eat their leftovers.

QUICK STATS

HABITAT:
Northern Europe, North America, Asia, Greenland

FOOD:
Grasses, lichen, mushrooms

SIZE:
5.6 feet long

WEIGHT:
700 pounds

LIFE EXPECTANCY:
15 years

Long Migrations

Caribou gather in large herds, and each summer they migrate nearly 600 miles to feed on grasses, mushrooms, and other plants. The food they consume in the summer will help them gain fat and prepare for the winter. If caribou stayed in the same place during the winter months, the caribou would have to endure harsh conditions. Instead, in the winter they migrate to a different area where food, snow fall, and weather aren't as harsh.

REINDEER OR CARIBOU?

Known for leading Santa's sleigh on Christmas, caribou, or reindeer, depending on where they're found in the world, are large members of the deer family. They live in northern tundra and taiga regions. Unlike other animals with antlers, both male *and* female caribou have antlers. Each year, they shed their antlers and grow new ones. The front of their antlers has a paddle shape that helps them scrape away ice and snow.

KILLER WHALE?

Orcas are often mistakenly called killer whales, but they are actually a member of the dolphin family. These marine mammals are known for their black and white coloring. Like penguins' coloring, orcas blend into the water when there is speckled sunlight and shadowing. Orcas, like their dolphin family members, are very intelligent and social creatures. They live in pods of up to 40 orcas and use clicks, squeaks, and whistles to communicate with one another. They also use echolocation for hunting and navigating.

QUICK STATS

HABITAT:
Cold, coastal waters around the world

FOOD:
Seals, sea lions, whales, fish, squid, sea birds

SIZE:
Up to 32 feet long

WEIGHT:
6 tons

LIFE EXPECTANCY:
80 years

Top of the Food Chain

Orcas are apex predators, meaning they don't have any predators except humans. Because of their sizable bodies, orcas eat around 550 pounds of food each day. Their mouths are lined with sharp teeth that are each 4 inches long! Orcas work together in groups to hunt. Like sheepdogs, members in a group surround a school of fish, taking turns to swim under the school in a coordinated orca carousel. They push the school of fish up to the surface of the water. Once the school is under control, one orca slams the school with their tail sending fish in the air and into orcas' mouths.

SOARING OVER SNOW

QUICK STATS

HABITAT:
Arctic

FOOD:
Lemmings, rabbits, rodents, birds, fish

SIZE:
Up to 28 inches with a 4.8-foot wingspan

WEIGHT:
Up to 6.5 pounds

LIFE EXPECTANCY:
10 years

Perching for hours, snowy owls inhabit the icy northern regions of North America, Europe, and Asia. Unlike other owls that are nocturnal, snowy owls are diurnal, meaning they are active at day or night.
With sharp vision and hearing, snowy owls can stay in the same spot for hours waiting for prey. Their hearing is so sensitive that they can hear their prey hidden under snow or vegetation. Once they capture their prey, they swallow them whole.

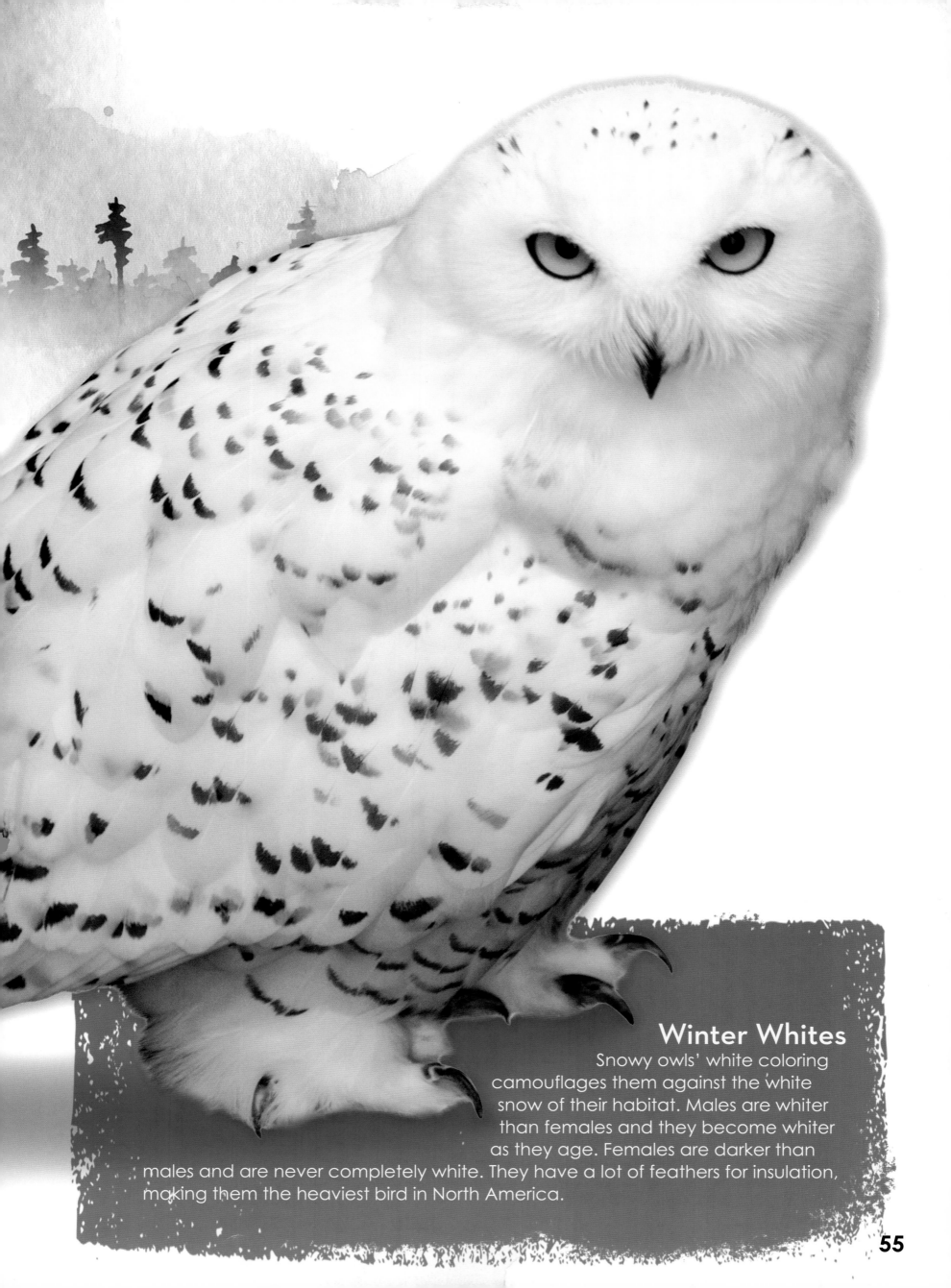

Winter Whites

Snowy owls' white coloring camouflages them against the white snow of their habitat. Males are whiter than females and they become whiter as they age. Females are darker than males and are never completely white. They have a lot of feathers for insulation, making them the heaviest bird in North America.

DON'T BE A RATTLE-TAIL!

QUICK STATS

HABITAT:
Valleys, grasslands, mountains of North America and South America

FOOD:
Mice, rats, squirrels, some birds

SIZE:
Up to 8 feet long

WEIGHT:
Up to 10 pounds

LIFE EXPECTANCY:
Up to 25 years

With a total of 24 species, rattlesnakes are some of the most recognizable snakes in the world—mostly because of the segmented rattle on the end of their tails used to warn predators of their presence. Their rattles are made of keratin, a protein that makes up hair and nails. At dusk, rattlesnakes begin looking for prey. Their forked tongue is flicked to pick up any of their prey's odors. Rattlesnakes even have a special organ on the roof of their mouth, called the Jacobson's organ, that is used for smelling. In addition, they have heat-sensitive pits on the sides of their head that can detect the heat of nearby prey. Without ears and with poor eyesight, the rattlesnake's tongue and heat-sensitive pits enable them to be expert hunters.

Potent Poison
When prey is close, rattlesnakes lunge and bite and inject venom from their fangs into their prey. The prey is able to run away, but the rattlesnake's stellar sense of smell guides the rattlesnake to the dying prey. However, not all animals are affected by the rattlesnake's venom. The king snake, the most widespread snake species in the United States, is immune to the rattlesnake's venom making rattlesnakes one of the king snake's favorite meals!

QUICK STATS

HABITAT:
Deserts of southwestern United States and northern Mexico

FOOD:
Birds' eggs, rodents, frogs, insects

SIZE:
Up to 21.5 inches long

WEIGHT:
Up to 3 pounds

LIFE EXPECTANCY:
20 years in the wild

With a bulky body, sharp claws, and venom, it's no surprise that this desert dweller is called a monster! Primarily found in the southwestern United States and northern Mexico, the Gila monster is one of two poisonous lizards in the world. Named after the Gila River in Arizona where they were discovered, Gila monsters have beadlike scales called osteoderms. The orange, pink, and yellow hues of the Gila monsters' skin helps them blend into the desert sand. The Gila monster has a powerful, venomous bite in which they can clamp on tightly to their prey for up to 15 minutes. While biting down, they also gnaw on their prey releasing venom into the wound.

Dining in the Desert

Although Gila monsters can be seen scaling saguaro cacti searching for birds eggs, it is not uncommon for Gila monsters to only eat several meals a year. Gila monsters store fat in their tail to sustain them when food is scarce. They also spend 95 percent of their time underground and rarely emerge to look for food.

DESERT DRAGON

ONE HUMP
OR TWO?

Unlike their Arabian cousins that have one hump, Bactrian camels have two humps and live in the deserts and steppes of China and Mongolia. Contrary to popular belief, the camels' humps do not store water, but rather fat, for later use. Since food can be scarce in the desert, camels can use the energy from the fat in their humps. Bactrian camels can go about a week without water and several months without food. Temperatures in the desert can be harsh with scorching heat in the summer and freezing temperatures in the winter. Because of this, Bactrian camels grow a thick, shaggy coat to keep warm in the winter that they later shed in the summer.

HABITAT:
Dry grasslands and deserts of China and Mongolia

FOOD:
Shrubs, grasses, plants

SIZE:
11.5 feet long, 5.9 feet tall

WEIGHT:
1,800 pounds

LIFE EXPECTANCY:
Up to 40 years

Made for Life in the Desert

Because of swirling sands, camels have special features that help them live in the desert. On their face, they have a special clear, inner eyelid that helps them see and protects their eyes from sand and dirt. They also have double rows of long eyelashes and bushy eyebrows that also protect their eyes. Camels' big, flat feet help them navigate through soft and shifting sand. Their nostril slits can also close so they don't breathe in sand.

QUICK STATS

HABITAT:
Deserts and grasslands
of every continent except
Antarctica

FOOD:
Insects, spiders, worms

SIZE:
8 inches

WEIGHT:
3.5 ounces

LIFE EXPECTANCY:
5 years

Hold on Tight, Babies!

Scorpion moms have up to 100 babies at a time. Unlike their spider relatives, scorpions don't lay eggs. Instead, they give birth to live young that emerge white in color and with soft exoskeletons. In order to get around, the babies hop on their mom's back for up to 20 days. Then they leave their mom's back and get around on their own.

With bodies covered in armor, two large pincers, and a sharp spike on their tail, scorpions are fierce desert predators. Scorpions are arachnids, like spiders, and have eight legs. During the day, most scorpions rest in burrows and come out to hunt at night. They grab their prey with their pincers, and then sting them with their telson, the poisonous tip of their tail. Each type of scorpion species has different venom that is effective on their prey of choice.

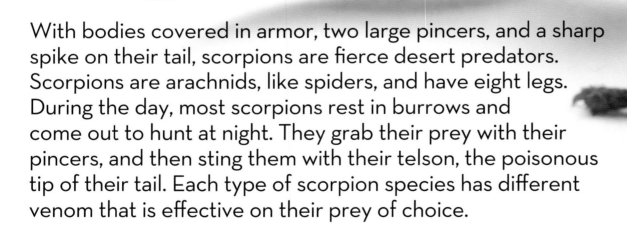

DESERT
DEFENSE

NATURE'S NIGHTMARE

Big, hairy, with lots of legs—it may seem like a science fiction monster, but tarantulas are one of the most widespread spiders around the world. Unlike their spider relatives, tarantulas don't spin webs to capture their prey. Instead, they wait for their prey to approach, and then they grab it with their appendages.

Tarantulas inject venom into their prey, and it's about as powerful as bee venom. Since tarantulas don't have big mouths with lots of teeth to chew their prey, they secrete a special digestive enzyme that liquefies their prey so they can be sucked up through their straw-like mouth opening.

Coming Out of Their Skin

Like snakes that shed their skin, tarantulas shed, or molt, their external skeleton once a year. Before they shed, a new, larger skeleton develops under the skeleton they are about to molt. After a few hours, the tarantula has shed its external skeleton, and the new, visible skeleton is soft and vulnerable until it hardens.

QUICK STATS

HABITAT:
All continents except Antarctica

FOOD:
Insects, frogs, toads, mice

SIZE:
Up to 11 inches

WEIGHT:
3 ounces

LIFE EXPECTANCY:
Up to 30 years

QUICK STATS

HABITAT:
Deserts and semi-deserts of North and Central America from Southern Canada to Guatemala

FOOD:
Ants and other insects

SIZE:
Up to 6 inches

WEIGHT:
0.2 ounces

LIFE EXPECTANCY:
Up to 5 years

Seeing Red

Covered in spines with a crown of horns on their heads, horned toads don't look like the most appetizing snack. However, predators such as coyotes still attempt to eat these spiky lizards. Luckily, horned toads have several defense mechanisms to protect themselves. Similar to puffer fish in the ocean, horned toads have the ability to inflate their bodies so they are twice their normal size and harder to eat. The most mysterious defense mechanism is shooting blood out of their eyes to scare off predators! When they sense a predator, pouches inside their eyes begin filling with blood, allowing them to shoot blood up to three feet. This strategy isn't necessarily dangerous to predators—instead it confuses the predator giving the horned toad time to escape.

DESERT DRAGON

Horned toads may resemble a fire-breathing dragon or even a dinosaur, but these lizards are mostly harmless. Because of their blunt snout, they are called toads, but they are really lizards. Unlike most streamlined lizards, horned toads have wide bodies that make them more difficult for predators to eat. Their short and stout bodies also make them quite slow.

They camp out in front of an ant hole and eat ants as they walk in front of them. Because their diet mostly consists of ants, horned toads need to eat a lot of them, so their stomach makes up a large percentage of their body.

From southern Canada to northern Mexico, bighorn sheep can be seen scaling steep, rocky mountains. Bighorn sheep are related to goats and have similar split hooves that help them grip rocks and dirt so they can climb to places that most predators can't get to. Their wideset eyes provide bighorn sheep with a better field of vision to look out for predators. The large horns on the males' heads can weigh up to 30 pounds—as much as the rest of the bones in the bighorn sheep's body. Females also have horns, but they are much smaller and only slightly curved.

EXPERT MOUNTAIN CLIMBERS

Hitting Horns

Female bighorn sheep, called ewes, live in groups of up to 15 with baby bighorn sheep. Bachelor groups of male bighorn sheep, or rams, come into contact with ewes only when it's time to mate. The males' large, curved horns come in handy when it's time to fight for a mate. Males lock and hit horns to show their dominance so they can win over a potential mate.

QUICK STATS

HABITAT:
Southwestern Canada, southwestern United States, and Northern Mexico

FOOD:
Grasses, plants

SIZE:
6 feet long, 3.5 feet tall

WEIGHT:
Up to 300 pounds

LIFE EXPECTANCY:
14 years

HOOO IS THAT FLYING AT NIGHT?

QUICK STATS

HABITAT:
Every continent except Antarctica

FOOD:
Insects, small rodents, small birds, fish

SIZE:
28 inches tall

WEIGHT:
Up to 9 pounds

LIFE EXPECTANCY:
20 years

Made for the Night

When the moon and stars are out, owls can be found hooting and looking for their next meal. Owls have large eyes that help them see in the dark. They can't move their eyes, however, instead they can turn their heads 270 degrees in each direction. Owls have good hearing and can hear a mouse stepping on a twig 75 feet away!

Owls are birds of prey—birds with sharp beaks and talons, like eagles and hawks. Unlike other birds of prey, owls are mostly nocturnal so they can share a territory with eagles and hawks, which are active during the day.

Owls are typically found alone in nests that have been made by other birds or on the ground in burrows. When they are in groups, a group of owls is called a parliament, named after C. S. Lewis' *The Chronicles of Narnia*, in which there's a scene with a meeting of owls.

WHITE TAIL, WHITE SPOTS

At dusk and dawn, it's not uncommon to see white-tailed deer browsing meadows in the summer, and forests in the winter. In the summer, white-tailed deer are a reddish-brown color, and in winter they turn a gray-brown color.

Fawns, or baby deer, have brown coats with white spots that camouflage them in the forest. The white spots look like speckled sunlight. White-tailed deer are named after the white underside of their tails, that they lift when they are startled.

QUICK STATS

HABITAT:
Forests and meadows from Canada to South America

FOOD:
Leaves, twigs, fruit, nuts, grass

SIZE:
7.75 feet long

WEIGHT:
Up to 300 pounds

LIFE EXPECTANCY:
14 years

Showing Off

Male deer, called bucks, have antlers that grow on their head each year. Their antlers are grown in the spring and are covered in a soft material called velvet. As the antlers continue to grow, the velvet rubs off. In winter, the bucks shed their antlers. Males use their antlers to defend their territory, show dominance, and fight other males for a mate.

QUICK STATS

HABITAT:
Wooded areas all over the world except Australia

FOOD:
Insects, fruit, nuts, acorns

SIZE:
19-inch body,
30-inch wingspan

WEIGHT:
12.3 ounces

LIFE EXPECTANCY:
11 years

Thump, thump, thump . . . woodpeckers are birds with extremely strong beaks that they use to hammer into trees. They peck tree bark looking for insects, fruit, nuts, and acorns to eat.

Once they find a delicious snack, they stick their long tongue—up to 4 inches long—into the cavity. The end of their tongue is covered with a sticky substance that helps them grab their food. In the forest, it's not uncommon to hear constant pecking. A woodpecker can peck 10,000 to 12,000 holes in trees in just one day!

Extra Protection

With constant pecking, it's no surprise that woodpeckers have extra protection in their heads to protect their brains. Their brain is surrounded by a spongy skull, and their long tongue wraps back into their head and acts like a cushion around the brain.

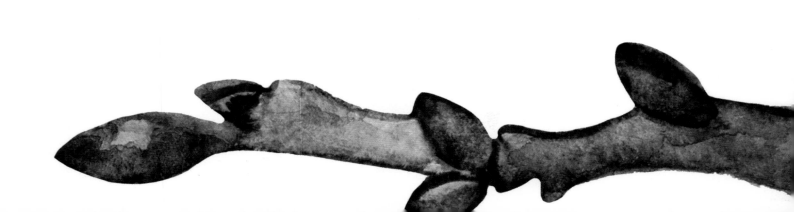

WHAT'S THAT NOISE?

BROWN BEAR, BROWN BEAR, WHAT DO YOU SEE?

Part of the brown bear species, grizzly bears can be found in the interior of North America. Their fur coloring is brown with white tips, which is how they got their name "grizzly," which means streaked with gray. Grizzlies are solitary—only females and their cubs are seen together. They communicate with sounds, movements, and smells. Some grizzlies will rub their back against a tree truck to let other grizzlies know they were there!

QUICK STATS

HABITAT:
Interior of North America

FOOD:
Nuts, berries, fish, rodents, deer, moose

SIZE:
8 feet

WEIGHT:
800 pounds

LIFE EXPECTANCY:
25 years

Good Night, Sleep Tight

Beginning in the summer, female grizzlies begin eating large, hearty meals in order to build up fat. They'll need this fat during their winter den hibernation that can last up to six months.

Grizzlies have extra sharp claws that they use to dig their dens. Each den includes an entrance, short tunnel, and chamber. During hibernation, some females give birth to babies—often two cubs that are twins.

MASKED BANDITS

Known for their masked face and ringed tail, raccoons live in woodlands, grasslands, and even cities. Although there are many theories regarding their signature mask, many experts believe the markings make their eyes look bigger or reduce glare in their eyes. When raccoons have babies, called kits, they are born with their distinctive black mask.

QUICK STATS

HABITAT:
Grasslands, forests, cities, towns of North America

FOOD:
Fruit, berries, small mammals, insects, fish

SIZE:
37.5 inches

WEIGHT:
23 pounds

LIFE EXPECTANCY:
3 years

Hungry Hunters

Raccoons are one of few animals that examine and clean their food before eating it. They use their hands for grabbing frogs and fish out of rivers and lakes, grabbing leftovers from trash cans, and picking apart their food before eating it.

In fact, the word raccoon is based on a Native American Powhatan word meaning "animal that scratches with its hands."

BIG, BAD WOLF

Wolves may seem scary, but they're actually related to dogs, like those we keep as pets such as golden retrievers or German shepherds. Wolves are social animals that live in packs. Packs typically include an alpha male and female and their offspring.

They use many techniques to keep in touch with one other such as growls, barks, scent, body language, and of course, howling. Wolves howl to communicate with their pack over long distances or to vocalize excitement. Each wolf has a distinctive howl that tells them apart—similar to human fingerprints.

QUICK STATS

HABITAT:
Europe, Alaska, Canada, Asia

FOOD:
Deer, elk, moose, small mammals, fish, lizards, snakes

SIZE:
63 inches long, 20-inch tail

WEIGHT:
175 pounds

LIFE EXPECTANCY:
8 years

Playful Pups

When wolf babies, or pups, are born their mother nurses the pups while other members of the pack hunt and bring back food. After a few weeks, pups begin playing, wrestling, and learning skills from the older members of the pack.

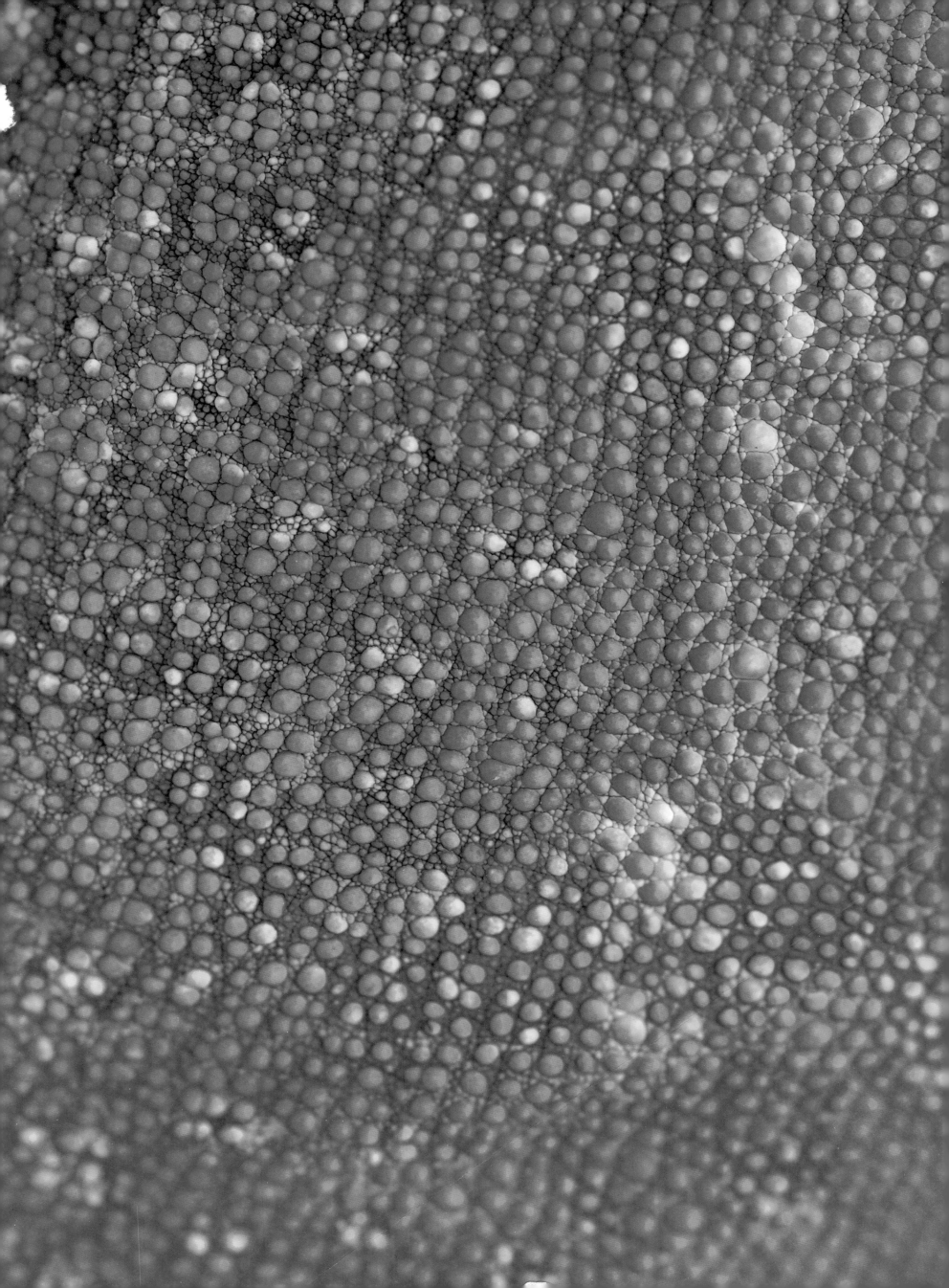